A THOUSAND MILES TO
BAGHDAD

Impressions & Images
From Two Journalists
Embedded with U.S. Marines

Photography by HAYNE PALMOUR IV • Text by DARRIN MORTENSON

Published by NORTH COUNTY TIMES
A Division of Lee Enterprises

FRONT COVER: Lance Cpl. Joshua Zeller, of Roll, Arizona, is overwhelmed by a raucous crowd of Iraqis in Saddam City on April 10, 2003. Thousands of Iraqis filled the streets to greet the Marines as they established themselves in Baghdad with little resistance. Trained and equipped for a combat mission, the Marines suddenly faced peacekeeping, humanitarian, and police roles when they arrived in Baghdad.

PAGE 1: Lance Cpl. Jonathan Garcia, 20, of Puerto Rico pokes his head above his foxhole after Iraqis launched Scud missiles at Marines camped along the Kuwait/Iraq border. The warheads did not contain chemical weapons and no one was reported killed or injured by the attacks, but the threat kept Marines on edge as they waited for the order to invade. (March 20)

RIGHT: As the invasion begins, Cpl. Armando Davila, 21, of The Dalles, Oregon, peers down the trench that separates Kuwait and Iraq. The Marines had waited months for the order to cross what they called the "Line of Departure." (March 21)

ISBN: 1-59152-006-1
Photographs and text © 2003 *North County Times*, a division of Lee Enterprises

For more information write: North County Times, 207 E. Pennsylvania Ave., Escondido, CA 92025. Or call (760) 839-3333. Visit our website at: www.nctimes.com

NORTH COUNTY TIMES

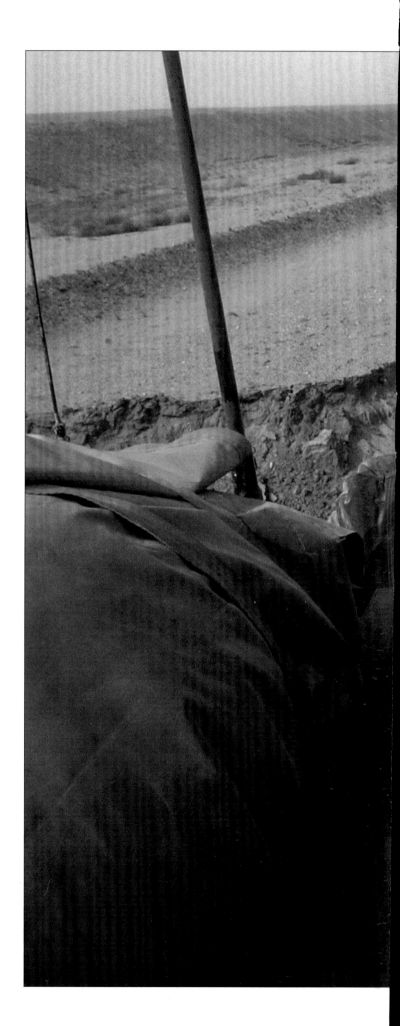

RIGHT: At dawn on March 21, 2003, members of the 3rd Battalion, 1st Marine Regiment crossed the "Line of Departure" and headed north to destroy the Baghdad Division of the Iraqi Republican Guard in Al Kut. The Baghdad Division collapsed before the Marines arrived, and fierce Iraqi resistance in the south forced the 3/1 to retrace its steps. The battalion finally arrived in Baghdad on April 6.

BELOW: Grimy and exhausted, Lance Cpl. Brian "Jeremy" Combs, foreground, and Cpl. James Reger, background, rest after a nearly 20-hour march from eastern Iraq to the Tigris River. Soot from diesel exhaust coated the Marines who rode in the amphibious assault vehicles. (April 4)

FACING PAGE: A Marine's war souvenir, a portrait of Iraqi President Saddam Hussein, leans against the track of an amphibious assault vehicle in a former Iraqi army training camp near Diwaniyah. (April 23)

CONTENTS

SAN DIEGO 11,000 m.
CALIFORNIA
Summersville, MO.
13,084 m.
RIFLE 10,100 m
COLORADO
KALAMAZOO 8940 m
MICHIGAN
BROWNSVILLE, TX
Hasta La Chingada

PREFACE

THE MARINES ARE AS MUCH A PART OF Southern California as surfers and sunshine. They train here, they eat here, they love here, and they sleep here.

When the United States sends its troops abroad, whether to keep the peace or to make war, the Marines go first. And the region goes with them.

Such was the case with the war in Iraq. Both of them.

But unlike the first Gulf War, when the government tethered the media to a short leash, the Pentagon slackened its hold for the second round with Iraqi President Saddam Hussein and invited journalists to "embed" with the troops: to sleep wherever whenever, to eat prepackaged meals, to wear unwashed clothes, to risk injury, even death.

The I Marine Expeditionary Force would lead the invasion. The 45,000-strong unit is based at Camp Pendleton, a 125,000-acre military reservation about 30 miles north of San Diego that is home to 90,000 service members and 10,000 civilian workers. It's our base; we've covered it since it opened in 1942. And we wanted to be with the troops in Iraq.

So we sent two of our finest journalists, reporter Darrin Mortenson and photographer Hayne Palmour.

They spent 77 days in the Middle East, leaving San Diego on Valentine's Day 2003 and returning 11 weeks later.

They hooked up with Lima Company, one of three rifle companies anchored with the 3rd Battalion, 1st Marine Regiment, 1st Marine Division. It's a storied battalion, nicknamed "The Thundering Third" for its heroic deeds in earlier wars.

We didn't expect Darrin and Hayne to report "the big picture." We left that job to *The New York Times*, The Associated Press, and other major news agencies.

We wanted our guys to tell stories. What did the Marines think? What did they see? What did they do?

Despite satellite transmission difficulties, equipment malfunctions, sandstorms, swarming flies, and gunfire, Darrin filed dozens of stories and Hayne sent hundreds of photographs.

This book is not a full accounting of their work; that's a later project. Rather, this book captures images, glimpsed, as Darrin writes, while "rolling through ancient Mesopotamia in the back of a 21st-century killing machine."

—Teresa Hineline, Assistant Managing Editor for News, and Cyndy Sullivan, Photo Editor, *North County Times*

ABOVE: Author Darrin Mortenson, left, and photographer Hayne Palmour use a satellite phone to file a story at a roadside camp near Al Hayy, Iraq. A small power inverter in the truck to the right kept the journalists' computer, camera, and phone batteries charged throughout the war. (March 29)

FACING PAGE: Homesick Marines post signs pointing the way home from Camp Tarawa, Kuwait, in early March.

When I give the word, together we will cross the Line of Departure …
—Maj. Gen. James Mattis

ABOVE: Maj. Gen. James Mattis, commander of the 1st Marine Division in Kuwait and Iraq, briefs a group of embedded journalists at the division's field headquarters at Camp Matilda in Kuwait. "You'll be livin' ugly and smellin' like a billy goat," he promised them. He kept his promise. (March 11)

RIGHT: Navy Corpsman Robert Cardona, 21, of Los Angeles reads a letter written by Maj. Gen. James Mattis. (March 18)

FACING PAGE: In a letter distributed to Marines just hours before they moved to the invasion staging area near the border, Maj. Gen. James Mattis calls the Marines to war. (March 18)

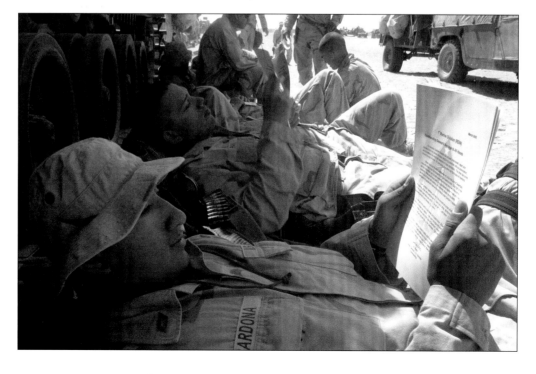

1ˢᵗ Marine Division (REIN)

Commanding General's Message to All Hands

For decades, Saddam Hussein has tortured, imprisoned, raped and murdered the Iraqi people; invaded neighboring countries without provocation; and threatened the world with weapons of mass destruction. The time has come to end his reign of terror. On your young shoulders rest the hopes of mankind.

When I give you the word, together we will cross the Line of Departure, close with those forces that choose to fight, and destroy them. Our fight is not with the Iraqi people, nor is it with members of the Iraqi army who choose to surrender. While we will move swiftly and aggressively against those who resist, we will treat all others with decency, demonstrating chivalry and soldierly compassion for people who have endured a lifetime under Saddam's oppression.

Chemical attack, treachery, and use of the innocent as human shields can be expected, as can other unethical tactics. Take it all in stride. Be the hunter, not the hunted: never allow your unit to be caught with its guard down. Use good judgement and act in best interests of our Nation.

You are part of the world's most feared and trusted force. Engage your brain before you engage your weapon. Share your courage with each other as we enter the uncertain terrain north of the Line of Departure. Keep faith in your comrades on your left and right and Marine Air overhead. Fight with a happy heart and strong spirit.

For the mission's sake, our country's sake, and the sake of the men who carried the Division's colors in past battles-*who fought for life and never lost their nerve*-carry out your mission and *keep your honor clean*. Demonstrate to the world there is "No Better Friend, No Worse Enemy" than a U.S. Marine.

J.N. Mattis
Major General, U.S. Marines
Commanding

ABOVE: Pfc. Joey Flowers, 22, of Newcastle, Oklahoma cleans grit from his fingernails while sitting in his foxhole in Camp Coyote, Kuwait, in late February. More than the discomforts and dangers of the war, Marines complained most of waiting and having nothing to do. (February 19)

FACING PAGE: A Marine guides a truck through a blinding sandstorm into Camp Inchon, Kuwait. Unable to see even a few feet in front of him, he passed the entrance several times before finally finding a way in. (March 12)

THE WAIT

On your young shoulders rest the hopes of mankind.
—Maj. Gen. James Mattis

THE MASSIVE BEDOUIN TENT LEAKED SAND from every seam. Its canvas walls flapped like sails as the storm ripped through the northern Kuwaiti desert, where tens of thousands of U.S. Marines camped, waiting to invade Iraq.

The sudden sandstorm seemed specially ordered to test us.

As the fine powder swept in waves across the plywood floor, I could barely make out the Marine officers huddled under their sleeping bags; my goggles and the flickering fluorescent lights did little to help.

Venturing out into the night with a notebook and pen, I could hardly see where to step, much less take notes. The Marines inside yelled at me for opening the flap, which I quickly closed, but not before clouds of dust whooshed inside.

The wind snatched everything that wasn't tied down, and the sand buried the things that were. It was blowing so hard that a Marine struggling to save gear from a collapsed tent was caught sideways by a gust and tumbled by me like a bag in the wind. I went back inside before I was next.

This was one of the desert's many moods.

"The shitters blew over, sir," a lance corporal blurted to one of the officers. Both of them blinked against the dust sprinkling down from the roof of the tent. A row of newly installed port-o-johns had just toppled. It was funny, but nobody laughed.

Outside, several Marines were lost in the storm.

My reporting partner, staff photographer Hayne Palmour, was out there, too. He was on his way back from photographing Marines practicing night maneuvers when the storm swept across our patch of desert. A Marine got out and guided their truck on foot, but they circled the camp several times before locating the entrance.

When Hayne finally stepped into our tent, he and his cameras were plastered with talc-like dust.

"Hayne, you look like a sugar cookie," said Lt. Col. Lew Craparotta, 3rd Battalion, 1st Marine Regiment's commander. This time we laughed.

When morning finally arrived and calm returned, we all looked like we'd been rolled in flour. The gritty dust coated our teeth and caked our eyes, noses, and ears. We dusted ourselves off and shook out our bedrolls and hawked up crunchy balls of mud — what one Marine called "dirt clods."

"Are you sure you guys wanna stick around with us out here?" Craparotta taunted.

Come wind or come sand, the answer was "yes."

Like the Marines, we were waiting for war.

For weeks we had been living easy in a hotel in Kuwait City, doing what we could to get access to Marine units in the field and keep up with the massive military machine building in the desert.

Every chance we got, we'd leave our comfortable digs at the Marriott in Kuwait City and tear north up Highway 80 to meet our Marine guides at a roadside marker — a clandestine gateway to one of the many growing military camps about 25 miles from the Iraq border.

Highway 80 is a desolate four-lane track through the moonscape of northern Kuwait to the border with Iraq. It is the same route on which Iraqi troops fled the country in 1991 after their brutal six-month occupation of Kuwait. People dubbed it the "Highway of Death" after allied warplanes trapped more than a thousand vehicles and the fleeing Iraqis inside them. Warplanes strafed and bombed them for hours, incinerating thousands.

Now, 12 years later, the highway was the main artery pumping men and materiel to the Marine Expeditionary Force. And Hayne and I were driving it daily, hoping for a chance to document America's next and, perhaps, final duel with Saddam Hussein.

We finally got our chance a week before the invasion, hooking up with Craparotta's Thundering Third from Camp Pendleton, California, in mid-March.

After nearly a month of waiting, we gladly surrendered our independence and relative safety, and forgot about clean sheets, hot showers, and salmon breakfasts in Kuwait City.

We traded it all for cold rations, Marines, sand, and uncertainty.

We were embedded.

ABOVE: Newly embedded reporters get a dose of military "hurry up and wait" as they sit crammed in the back of a truck on the way to meet their host units. (March 12)

FACING PAGE: A full moon shines over Liberation Tower in Kuwait City as residents prepare for war. Construction on the 1,220-foot-tall building, the tallest in the Middle East, was interrupted for three years after Iraq invaded Kuwait in August 1990. Construction resumed after U.S. and Coalition forces routed Iraqi forces in 1991. In 1996, when the tower was finally completed, the Kuwaiti government named it Liberation Tower to celebrate the country's comeback. (February 16)

ABOVE: Marines juggle a soccer ball as the sun sets at Camp Inchon, Kuwait. The Marines did their best to keep fit and busy in the final weeks before the invasion. (March 14)

LEFT: Lance Cpl. Todd Baker, 21, peers at the scab forming over the site where he received a smallpox inoculation. Marines had to monitor their painful wounds, keep them clean in the field, and then safely dispose of the scabs when they finally fell off. (February 19)

BELOW: A Marine infantryman tends to his feet at a training camp in Camp Coyote, Kuwait. The Marines often wore the same socks for four or more days, until they were crunchy and impermeable to sweat. The stench of rotting feet was one of the more memorable smells of war. (February 23)

ABOVE: Lance Cpl. Joshua Warren, left, and Cpl. Phillip Clark poke their heads from a foxhole to scan the flat desert around their positions at Camp Coyote, Kuwait. (February 19)

RIGHT: "Why am I here?" Marines debate their future role in Iraq with graffiti on a port-o-john wall at Camp Matilda in Kuwait. (March 14)

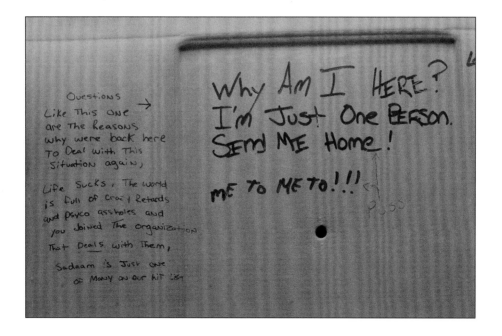

ABOVE: Cpl. Thomas Barnes takes an envious peek at a picture of a fellow Marine kissing his girlfriend when Kilo Company, 3rd Battalion, 5th Marine Regiment finally got mail in Kuwait. Once the war began on March 20, the Marines did not get mail for more than a month in Iraq. (February 23)

ABOVE: Lance Cpl. Tim Namovicz, 20, of Chicago writes a letter to his folks from Camp Coyote, Kuwait. "Been sittin' here so long just lookin' at blank stuff," he said of his life in the Kuwaiti desert. (February 19)

RIGHT: Marines pass another night with a smoke in a designated area outside the rows of Bedouin tents at Camp Inchon, Kuwait. Smoking and chewing tobacco were major pastimes for Marines in Kuwait and Iraq. (March 17)

ABOVE: Blowing off steam as they wait for the invasion, Marines play football in the sand at Camp Inchon, Kuwait. (March 14)

ABOVE: Staff Sgt. James Gerber struggles to keep the chickens alive at Camp Coyote, Kuwait. The fowl were used to detect chemical agents. Most of the chickens died from rough conditions, however, and were replaced with hardier pigeons, many of whom survived the war. (February 19)

RIGHT: Marines from the 3rd Battalion, 5th Regiment run in gas masks while training at Camp Coyote, Kuwait. (February 19)

ABOVE: Marines from the 1st Regimental Combat Team brush their teeth and take care of personal hygiene as the sun rises over Camp Inchon, Living Support Area 1, Kuwait. (March 18)

LEFT: Navy chaplain Cmdr. Bill Devine at the 5th Marine Regiment's camp in Kuwait. (February 22)

RIGHT: Lance Cpl. Peter Kruse, 21, of Chicago prays during a Protestant service just before he is baptized at Camp Inchon, Kuwait, two days before the Marines assembled at the border to invade Iraq. (March 16)

FACING PAGE: Marines listen to President Bush give Saddam Hussein a final ultimatum over a shortwave radio on a Humvee hood at Camp Inchon, Kuwait. (March 18)

CALL TO WAR

When I give you the word, together we will cross the Line of Departure,
close with those forces that choose to fight, and destroy them.
—Maj. Gen. James Mattis

THE TENT FLAP OPENED AND HEAVY BOOT-STEPS clomped across the dusty, plywood floor.

A fluorescent light buzzed and crackled as someone flipped it on, and the footsteps grew louder as they approached our end of the long Bedouin tent.

I didn't have to poke my head out of my sleeping bag to know what it was. No one did.

The only thing important enough to wake the colonel at that early hour was the call to war.

"Major Gideons, the order, sir," the Marine said, alerting the colonel's operations officer, Maj. Chris Gideons.

We were to move to the Iraq/Kuwait border later that day, March 18.

As we peeled back our sleeping bags and looked at each other, we knew this was the last time we'd wake up at Camp Inchon.

No one spoke as we packed our gear, except for a nervous "this is it," mumbled by a few Marines to no one in particular.

The Marines had been prepared for weeks. Vehicles were loaded and lined up in the order they would move across the desert. Ammunition was issued. Everybody was trained and retrained on the invasion plan.

But as we prepared to head into an uncertain fate, readiness was suddenly a deeply personal thing — for us and the Marines.

Waiting to cross the border hours before the ground war began, I would get a glimpse of how the Marines prepared spir-

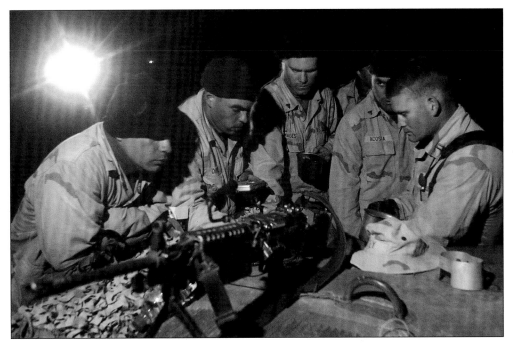

itually to face the prospect of death and killing and having no way to turn back.

In an ugly, forbidding patch of wasteland near the Iraq border, radioman Cpl. Armando Davila sent his fellow Marines scurrying for cover with three words: "Lightning! Lightning! Lightning!"

The Iraqis had launched several Scud missiles.

The alarm broke up a gathering of about 50 Marines who were attending a small Catholic Mass a mere leap and a roll away from freshly dug foxholes.

One of the holes was mine, another was Hayne's.

Navy Chaplain Wayne Haddad, in his Lenten vestments and gas mask, landed in my foxhole, along with his sidekick, Navy Chaplain's Assistant Manuel Ortiz.

"This is the land of Abraham …," Haddad had just told the troops minutes before the alert. "This is the land where the prophets were, and the world is still fighting over this land….The Scriptures come alive out here."

He was about to administer the Eucharist, the Catholic sacrament representing the body and blood of Jesus Christ, when the Scud alarm sent him scrambling for cover.

"Just one more second, Lord," he said under his quickened breath, peeling off his mask after the "all clear" was given. "Just one more minute and I would have been done."

Sitting in the hole, he said that his stock with the troops had gone up in recent days and that many had come to him with misgivings and questions about the war. This quiet little preacher from New Jersey really cared for his Marines.

"They are very ready. They're very confident," Haddad said.

He said that very few who came to talk to him were afraid for their personal safety. They were more worried about their families and their souls than themselves.

"What they want to know is, 'Where am I spiritually?'" Haddad said. "They want to know what that means for their spirituality if they go in and take someone's life."

"I always tell them that there is a difference between murder and killing in war," he said.

Haddad said he'd tell them it's OK with God if they kill in war because "He considers it self-defense."

"They're very relieved when I tell them that," he said.

I wondered if they were really relieved, or if they wished they could just turn back and not put themselves in the position to kill or be killed now that the first shots fired there were an unstoppable momentum toward something terrible.

I wasn't relieved. There was no turning back for me, either. There was no ride out of the desert, no way to call a timeout. No way to take it all back.

I thought of a poem by the Persian poet Rumi that I had heard years ago when I was confused and at a crossroads in my life.

Birds make great sky circles of their freedom.
How do they learn it?
They fall. And falling, they're given wings.

I was falling headlong into war.

RIGHT: Navy chaplain Lt. Cmdr. Tom Webber baptizes Cpl. Albert Martinez, 21, from Sunnyvale, California, in a sandbag-lined pool during a ceremony at Camp Inchon, Kuwait. As they readied for war and faced the possibility of dying, many Marines swore off drinking, womanizing, and other wicked ways. (March 16)

ABOVE: Marines scramble for cover after the "Lightning! Lightning! Lightning!" alert is given, warning of inbound Scud missiles. (March 20)

ABOVE: Marines from Lima Company, 3/1, move from Camp Inchon in Kuwait to the invasion assembly area near the Kuwait/Iraq border. (March 18)

LEFT: Marine Sgt. Brian Anderson watches the company pigeon for signs of airborne chemical agents during a Scud attack alert. Many of the pigeons survived the war and made it back to Kuwait with the Marines. (March 20)

ABOVE: Marines dig foxholes in the Iraqi desert after crossing the "Line of Departure." (March 22)

RIGHT: Cpl. Gunnar Schmitt, 23, of Janesville, Wisconsin, rests in his freshly dug foxhole as the sun sets over the invasion assembly area. (March 19)

BELOW: During an Iraqi Scud missile attack on U.S. bases in Kuwait, Cpl. Armando Davila drafts a pool for Marines to bet on the day they would return to San Diego. Many Marines expected a much longer conflict, and some placed bets on dates as late as July. Marines usually found some way to brighten even the darkest moments of the war. (March 20)

ABOVE: Marines from Lima Company, 3rd Battalion, 1st Marine Regiment prepare to move to the Kuwait/Iraq border just hours after President Bush made a speech giving Saddam Hussein 48 hours to flee Iraq. When they returned to the U.S. on May 23, they had been away from home most of a year. (March 18)

LIMA COMPANY

Be the hunter, not the hunted; never allow your unit
to be caught with its guard down.
—Maj. Gen. James Mattis

I NEVER MET CPL. ANTONIO "TONY" Sledd, but while traveling with Lima Company, I felt I knew him.

Suspected al-Qaida gunmen killed the 20-year-old from Tampa, Florida, while he was playing a game of stickball, unwinding after a day of training on a small Kuwaiti island in the Persian Gulf.

Lima and some of the other units from 3/1 were on the island as part of a routine, seven-month deployment in the region when the attackers killed Sledd and wounded another Marine. Lima's Marines shot back, killing two of the gunmen, who were dressed like civilian workers. That was in October 2002, five months before U.S. forces invaded Iraq.

But for Lima's "Warriors," as they called themselves, the bullet that killed Tony Sledd was the first shot of the war. And to those troops, the war was just one last mission before they could all go home.

For the duration of the war, I felt Sledd's spirit somehow guiding the Marines — watching their backs as they rolled through ambushes on the highways in the south and patrolled crowded Baghdad streets. Sledd's memory kept them alert, together, safe.

But I also sensed a darker influence: revenge.

I worried the Marines might try to avenge Sledd. It was a fear fed by Marine talk of "payback time."

Who would they pay back? I thought. The answer seemed to be "Hajis," what Marines routinely called

ABOVE: Boots, helmet, and rifle are a traditional memorial for a fallen Marine. This one on October 11, 2002 at Camp Pendleton is for Cpl. Antonio "Tony" Sledd, a Lima Company Marine who was killed by al-Qaida sympathizers five months before the U.S. invasion of Iraq.

Arabs, using a dehumanizing term the same way American soldiers used "gooks" and "dinks" to describe Asians in earlier conflicts in Korea and Vietnam.

Whether any of Lima's Marines ever let the memory of Sledd pull the trigger is something only they know. But Lima Company commander Capt. Matt Reid and other leaders never used Sledd's name as a battle cry, only as a warning. Reid often made subtle reference to Sledd,

reminding the Marines to watch their backs around Iraqi civilians and to never let down their guard.

Few ever talked directly about Sledd — the topic was taboo — but he was always there.

When the company returned from Iraq to its base at Camp Pendleton without losing a single man, Reid didn't recap their accomplishments or celebrate their victories.

He had some simple words.

"Don't forget about Corporal Sledd," he said. "I know he's up there watching us. Let's never forget that."

ABOVE: Lance Cpl. Brian "Jeremy" Combs waits in the back of the amphibious assault vehicle that carried Lima Company's officers and the author and photographer into Iraq. The Marines waited at this desolate spot for two nights before the order was given to invade. "My grandfather was in World War II. I had two uncles go to Vietnam. My cousin was in the Gulf," he said. "And now I'm here sittin' in this freakin' sandbox waiting to go to war." (March 20)

ABOVE: After a long patrol of Aziziyah, Iraq, some of Lima Company's officers joke and laugh recounting drunken exploits during deployments to Southeast Asia. From left: 1st Lt. Eli Vasquez, an artillery officer attached to Lima; 1st Lt. Bill Frank; 1st Lt. Donald Toscano; and Capt. John Chau, Lima Company's executive officer. (April 5)

LEFT: Staff Sgt. Roy Whitener surveys a Republican Guard weapons cache in an elementary school in Muwaffaqiyah, Iraq. Whitener was one of Lima Company's more experienced staff noncommissioned officers. (April 2)

ABOVE: Hours after the Marines left Baghdad, Lima Company's assault vehicles travel through a flock of sheep and negotiate furrows outside Al Hillah, Iraq, near the ruins of ancient Babylon. (April 21)

FACING PAGE: Residents of a small agricultural settlement outside Al Garaf in Iraq huddle in fear as Marines search their homes. This was one of the first personal encounters between 3/1 Marines and Iraqis during the war. (March 25)

ROLLING THROUGH MESOPOTAMIA

Share your courage with each other as we enter the uncertain terrain north of the Line of Departure.
—*Maj. Gen. James Mattis*

AS A KID I HAD OFTEN WANTED TO TRAVEL TO the land of the Bible and Ali Baba.

I just never expected to get there the way I did: on a Blitzkrieg charge in the back of an armored amphibious assault vehicle with a company of U.S. Marines.

But there we were, rumbling down the highway past dusty Bedouin camps, along green tributaries of the Euphrates and Tigris Rivers, across the Muslim heartland of southern Iraq.

We were rolling through ancient Mesopotamia in the back of a 21st-century killing machine.

On this trip, when East met West, when the old world encountered the new, the exchange was often limited to an uneasy wave or gunfire.

Inside the dark, noisy belly of the amphibious assault vehicle — or track — riding as part of a massive military convoy, we were insulated from the world outside.

We had our own food and purified our own water. We slept in fields and abandoned buildings away from Iraqis. We counted on the locals for nothing.

Most of the Marines did not even seem curious. Few talked about the place or the people.

They were in Iraq, thousands of miles from America, but their thoughts were clearly still on home.

First Lt. Eli Vasquez chattered about cheeseburgers and Texas. Cpl. Armando Davila got philosophical about Britney Spears' backside. Lance Cpl. Brian "Jeremy" Combs reviewed video games as he spat tobacco juice into a designer water bottle.

In the first days, as the invasion charged through the deserts of the south, the only Iraqis we saw were curious Bedouins who left their nomadic encampments to watch and wonder at the convoy of green military monsters snaking down the highway.

As we pushed through the farmlands of the mid-Euphrates plain, Arab women cloaked in black shuffled back to flat-roofed brick dwellings, disappearing inside until we rumbled past. People peered from windows and doorways.

Everything seemed a mystery. Their ways. Our ways.

Intentions were unclear. They hid, and we watched them closely — every one a potential enemy.

As the Iraqis gradually warmed to us, the Marines lightened up, but little, if anything, was learned or exchanged. Even up close, patrolling through crowds of cheering Iraqis in the streets of Baghdad, the gulf between history, language, and culture was usually too wide to cross in the middle of a war.

For some Marines, the extreme poverty, open sewers, and incomprehensible language were somehow reasons to hate and belittle the Iraqis. Others seemed humbled by being in the "Cradle of Civilization" and felt duty-bound to help the Iraqi people.

From the back of the track it was an impenetrable, incomprehensible world out there.

As an embedded reporter, I couldn't step away from the Marines to learn how the Iraqis felt about the invasion or about Americans.

Wearing the same uniform as a Marine, traveling in the track, and patrolling in formation, I was just another American soldier to the Iraqis. Honesty from the Iraqis was not something I expected under the circumstances. You tell men with guns whatever they want to hear. And I was with the men with guns.

I was left to wonder about a country where the only child's toy I saw was a plastic AK-47, and where we found a young woman chained to a wall.

I was left to wonder what the guerrillas were fighting for, and whether the small photos of Saddam Hussein I saw in almost every Iraqi bedroom were there because they had to be, or because Iraqis somehow loved their leader.

I was left to wonder if the Iraqis who cheered us on as we walked and rolled down the streets really welcomed America's invasion and occupation, or if they were waiting for the right time to unsheath their knives.

I would never know. The war stood in the way.

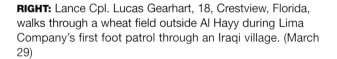

RIGHT: Lance Cpl. Lucas Gearhart, 18, Crestview, Florida, walks through a wheat field outside Al Hayy during Lima Company's first foot patrol through an Iraqi village. (March 29)

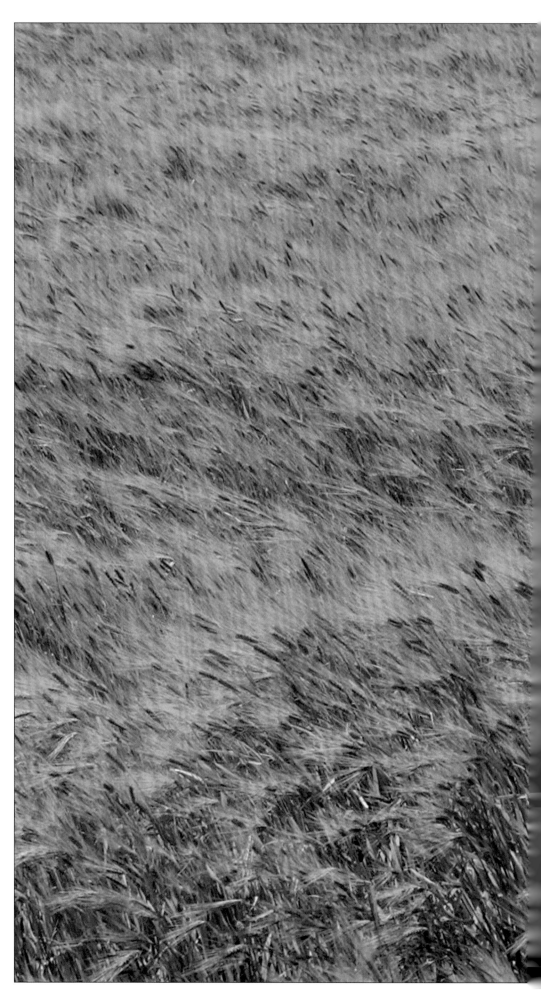

ABOVE: Marines from Lima Company barge into an Iraqi home during a house-to-house search of Muwaffaqiyah, near Al Kut, in Iraq. Marines typically confiscated weapons, uniforms, large amounts of cash, or military documents on such patrols. (April 2)

ABOVE: After being searched by one group of Marines, residents of Ash Shatra continue holding their hands on their heads as more Marines rush by in search of Saddam Fedayeen militia. (March 31)

LEFT: A Marine "clears" an Iraqi family's kitchen during a house-to-house search for weapons in Muwaffaqiyah, on the outskirts of Al Kut. Early in the war, Marines kicked in doors and ransacked rooms during the searches, but they later learned to make the searches less intrusive. (April 2)

ABOVE: A Marine frisks an Iraqi man who surrendered to Marines on the second day of the invasion. Large groups of scraggly Iraqi soldiers and civilians approached the Marines' convoy during the first few days of the war, most asking for food. (March 23)

BELOW: The 3rd Battalion stops along the route to An Nasiriyah, Iraq. Intense Iraqi resistance around the bridges across the Euphrates River in An Nasiriyah created a traffic jam that slowed the Marines' advance for days. (March 23)

ABOVE: Master Sgt. Keith La France, 53, looks out from the gun turret of Lima Company's command vehicle. La France, or "Top" as he was known, led Alpha Company, 4th Amphibious Assault Battalion — reservists from Norfolk, Virginia, who drove 3/1 to Baghdad and back. (March 22 or 23)

LEFT: Lima Company leads the 3rd Battalion's first foot patrol of an Iraqi settlement near Al Hayy. (March 29)

RIGHT: An Iraqi girl watches Marines on patrol in Saddam City. Boys and men usually ran out to greet the Marines, while women and girls hung back in doorways, windows, and on balconies. (April 10)

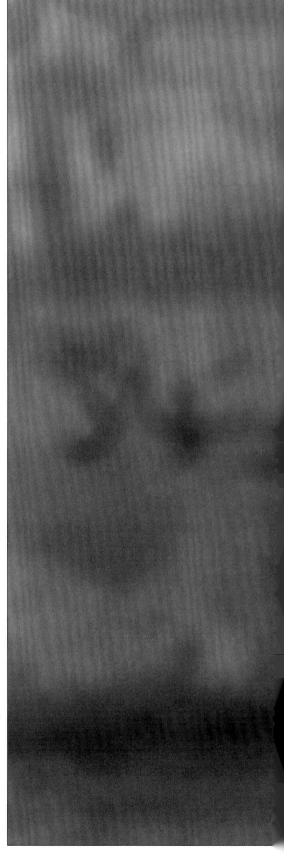

BELOW: This shot of a typical settlement in southern Iraq was taken from a CH-53 helicopter as the author and photographer headed back to Kuwait. (April 23)

ABOVE: During a break in a 20-hour road march to the Tigris River, weary Marines eat and rest. From front to back, Cpl. James Reger, Lance Cpl. Brian "Jeremy" Combs, and Gunnery Sgt. Jerry Yates. Reger, who had been awake for about 36 hours, spent most of the day repairing the assault vehicles. (April 4)

RIGHT: A baby camel saunters past Marines stopped in the desert north of the Iraq/Kuwait border. (March 22)

ABOVE: The highway north of An Nasiriyah was littered with buses, military vehicles, and privately owned vehicles destroyed by the advancing Marine forces. Many were clearly military. Many were not, however, and the bodies on the road often included women and children. (March 25)

LEFT: An Iraqi family watches as Marines search other Iraqis at a roadblock along the highway near Al Hayy. (March 27)

ABOVE: Marines wake up and prepare to "stand to" at dawn in the southern Iraqi desert. (March 23)

BELOW: Marines detonate an Iraqi arms cache at the edge of Aziziyah. The detonation and resulting "cook-off" explosions crumbled neighbors' walls and shattered windows for blocks, enraging many residents who had hailed the Marines during a patrol earlier that day. (April 5)

ABOVE: The language gap was deep and wide. Lima Company's executive officer Capt. John Chau, 30, of Beaverton, Oregon, struggles to communicate with a resident of Aziziyah by using a translation card issued to Marines before the war. No one in the battalion spoke Arabic, and only one civilian translator accompanied the unit while it was in Iraq. (April 5)

ABOVE: Marines try to calm an Iraqi family as they search a house during a surprise patrol of Ash Shatra. The Marines had actually by-passed Ash Shatra on March 26 but returned there on March 30 to rout Baath Party loyalists and militia who had ambushed Marine supply units on the highway outside of town. (March 31)

LEFT: Marines said they were amazed to see Iraqis waving and cheering at them, like this crowd outside Qal'at Sukkar, as they back-tracked south to protect supply lines. "It was weird. It was great. I didn't know what to think," said Master Sgt. Keith "Top" La France of the reception. "I waved and blew them kisses, but I kept my finger on the .50-cal." (March 30)

ABOVE: In the glow of a burning oil facility, artillery officer Lt. Eli Vasquez aims his rifle out of Lima Company's command vehicle as the battalion rolls into battle in An Nasiriyah minutes before a firefight broke out. (March 25)

FACING DEATH

You are part of the world's most feared and trusted force.
Engage your brain before you engage your weapon.
—*Maj. Gen. James Mattis*

HAYNE AND I WERE SCARED, AND THE MARINES knew it.

As the convoy rolled north into the outskirts of An Nasiriyah, we heard reports that as many as 50 Marines had been killed, wounded, or captured. And we were next in line to attempt a run through the town.

Lima Company and 3/1 would have to go first, staying in town to fight so the rest of the convoy could cross the Euphrates River and pass through town.

The Marines offered us a chance to switch vehicles and tag along with another unit that would follow. They gave us about two minutes to talk it over.

I knew I didn't want to leave the guys in Lima. I trusted them.

I think the decision was easier for me than it was for Hayne. As a former U.S. Army infantryman, I thought I had a sense of what was more or less dangerous.

But it seemed like suicide to Hayne. He said he wanted to go on the truck that would follow the next day.

I appealed to the professional in him and argued that he'd get much better photographs from the ground than a moving truck or Humvee. I also told him we'd make harder targets outside than in a vehicle.

I believed it, but it was selfish, and for the rest of the morning, as the battle raged around us, I prayed that I had not just killed my friend and colleague.

Just after midnight, several tanks clanked ahead, leading our convoy of tracks through the chilly darkness over the Euphrates River where the bridgeheads were guarded by battle-weary Marines.

I had never prayed to get picked for the assignment to cover the war in Iraq. In a rare moment of total submission, I just asked God to put me wherever I was supposed to be, and left it at that.

When I landed the job in late January, I took that as the answer. But now, as our track rolled across the bridge into An Nasiriyah, I wondered if I hadn't mistaken the response.

Seconds later, a firefight broke out.

Hayne gripped his cameras, and we both kept our heads down as green and red tracers flashed overhead. Hot brass shell-casings rained down on us, and gunpowder smoke burned our eyes and throats.

Lt. Eli Vasquez, a 26-year-old preacher's son from Corpus Christi, Texas, had seemed so innocent moments before, harping about the virtues of Whataburgers and the beauties of Texas. Seeing him standing above us, shooting at Iraqis, I felt like we had lost something, like there was no going back to whoever we had been on the other side of the river.

For almost nine hours the Marines fought snipers — both real and imagined — from their positions among the rubble in the dusty median. As Iraqi snipers tried to fire at the convoy, the Marines responded with coordinated attacks with machine guns and rifles, mortars and grenades.

Building facades crumbled and houses burned as the Marines fired from behind whatever bits of rubble and wreckage they could find. With the enemy firing from both sides of the road, every Marine had to trust the next man to watch his back. We trusted all of them.

It was chaotic and confusing, frightening, exhausting, and completely unforgettable.

Remarkably, everybody in the regiment made it through the city alive. Other units could not boast the same.

Toward the end of the day, I caught a glimpse of Hayne absorbed in his work. He was crouching down to shoot a picture of Lt. Harry Thompson spreading a white cloth over the charred body of a Marine who had been killed in combat two days before.

I paused and thanked God that it turned out alright for us.

RIGHT: The Marines expected a bloody fight as their assault vehicles rumbled into the smoking outskirts of An Nasiriyah. It was an intense ride, and these Lima Company Marines kept to themselves. (March 24)

BELOW: Radioman Lance Cpl. Brian Wescott hangs his head as the Marines near the battle in An Nasiriyah. "We're friggin' gonna run the gauntlet," said company commander Capt. Matt Reid as the men prepared to enter the town. (March 24)

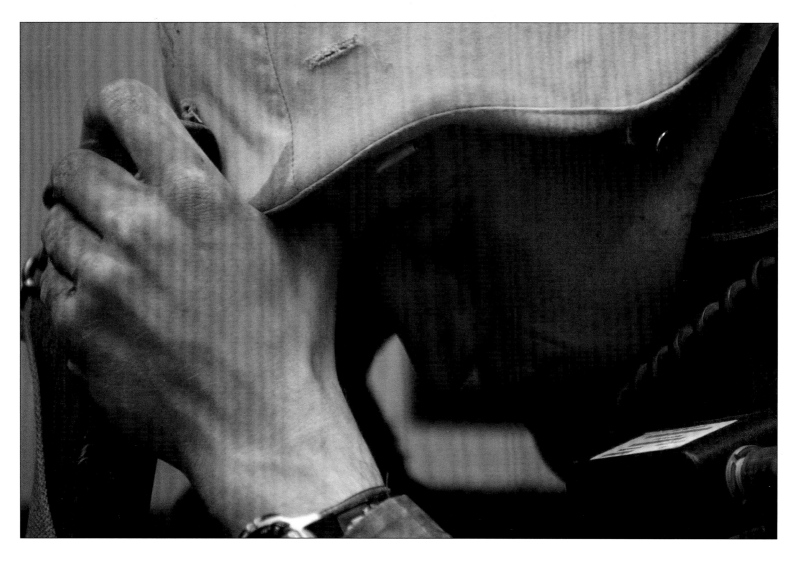

LEFT: Lima Company Marines dig in during a battle in An Nasiriyah. Third Battalion fought enemy snipers while the regimental convoy passed through town. (March 25)

ABOVE: Two Marines brave sniper fire in An Nasiriyah to recover a
.50-caliber machine gun and other parts from a disabled amphibious
assault vehicle. Both men survived. (March 25)

ABOVE: A Marine looks back warily as Lima Company battles snipers in An Nasiriyah. Marines had little, if any, cover in the dusty median and fought Iraqi snipers who were firing from buildings on both sides of the road. (March 25)

LEFT: A Marine shoots at snipers to provide cover for the rest of his unit in An Nasiriyah. The bits of metal and debris on the ground were mostly from an American amphibious assault vehicle that had been blown up by Saddam Fedayeen militia on March 23. At least four of the vehicles, and several trucks and Humvees, were disabled or destroyed by Iraqi forces in the previous few days. (March 25)

FOLLOWING PAGES: First Lt. Harry Thompson of Pennsylvania spreads an empty sandbag over part of the charred body of a Marine who was killed in battle in An Nasiriyah two days before. When they arrived in the pre-dawn darkness, edgy troops used the wreckage as cover from enemy fire. But as morning broke and the gore in the wreckage became clear, they eased away. "I just saw the trucks slowing down to take a look," Thompson said after covering the fallen Marine. "I just didn't think it was right. Those are Marines in there." (March 25)

ABOVE: In a tense moment in Qal'at Sukkar, two Iraqi civilians suddenly emerge from a building where Marines had battled snipers just minutes before. The man tried to kiss the Marines — an Arab demonstration of respect and submission — but the Marines were wary of his actions. (March 26)

THE FOG
OF WAR

*Our fight is not with the Iraqi people, nor is it with
members of the Iraqi army who choose to surrender.
—Maj. Gen. James Mattis*

THE "FOG OF WAR"—THE BLANKET OF FEAR AND uncertainty that settles on battlefields, often blurring the lines between civilian and combatant, friend and foe, right and wrong — hung over us the entire time we were in Iraq.

Beneath it lay bodies — the road north from An Nasiriyah was littered with them.

A black-robed man lay crumpled in the mud, a wood-stocked rifle by his side. Another one lay twisted at the end of a long set of footprints in the mud. It looked as if he'd been running away when he was taken down. A rocket-propelled grenade lay near-by. Over the highway shoulder leaned a civilian bus riddled with bullet holes, the mangled bodies of 16 dead Iraqi soldiers inside.

Not all the dead were fighters.

Some bodies hung from doors and windows of burning buses or lay in bloody heaps along the road. Among them were women and children.

Iraqi soldiers had mostly disappeared, shedding their uniforms and melting into the populace.

Some left soldiering and Saddam Hussein behind. But for others who stayed to fight, the clothes of a civilian were the perfect disguise.

Iraqi fighters pretending to surrender killed and wounded Marines in An Nasiriyah. And all along the route north, small teams of Iraqis in civilian dress ambushed the convoy — often after the main combat units had passed.

After the bloodshed in An Nasiriyah, the lead Marine units no longer gave Iraqis the benefit of the doubt just because they were wearing civilian clothes or traveling in private vehicles.

The Marines had good reason to be jumpy — the enemy could be anyone, anywhere — but I couldn't help wondering if leaving the roadways and towns strewn with dead Iraqi civilians wasn't a surefire way to inspire, rather than extinguish, Iraqi resistance.

That fog of war was particularly dense when we entered the town of Qal'at Sukkar on March 26. Only the day before, a massive sandstorm had halted the entire Marine Corps' advance.

The air was still grainy and the sky a yellow-gray from the dust as Lima moved in. Led by tanks, Lima's tracks barged into the town without warning, Marines firing at any likely sniper position or movement they saw in the houses or streets. The intrusion drew out some Iraqi fighters who started shooting back.

Hayne and I jumped out of the track and followed Capt. Matt Reid and his radioman, Cpl. Gunnar Schmitt, as they scrambled down the embankment to check the other platoons' positions. We ran crouched through the slick, stinking mud, trying to keep our heads below the level of the road.

From the road, the tracks' gunners blasted away with grenade launchers and machine guns. Marines lay in small teams along the embankment firing rifles and machine guns at movements in windows and alleyways. Brick and plaster walls crumbled, electric poles splintered and black smoke billowed from homes. When someone spotted movement on a rooftop, Marines pummeled the building with mortar fire, and we hit the dirt.

As we lay in the mud, Marines on both sides yelled that someone in the building behind us was shooting. I turned and saw what looked like a cluster of sandbags on one side of the roof. Through a railing, I could see something dart across the roof.

The Marines shot back. Troops howled and cheered as the green tracer rounds streaked across the field like laser beams and ricocheted when they hit the building's metal door. The barrage continued, starting and stopping several times.

When the Marines finally stopped firing, no more shots came from the building. Nothing seemed to move, but we waited and watched.

As the sun set, the sky turned orange as the light filtered through the sand still in the air after the storm. And as it quickly grew darker, a cold mist settled over the town. A chorus of crickets and croaking frogs, howling dogs, and braying donkeys echoed in the haze and seemed to taunt the Marines as they scanned the balconies and windows to our front and behind us.

Our imaginations went wild.

Then, in the last few minutes before the night and fog swallowed our view, an Iraqi man and woman popped through the metal door of the building the Marines had just blasted.

Marines started shouting and pointing their weapons at the two.

The man waved a white plastic bag and the woman wailed as they came toward us, first in slow starts, then in a full rush.

Some of the Marines pressed their faces behind the sights of their rifles, ready to shoot, when the man lunged at the troops, crying something in Arabic that we didn't understand.

Both sides jabbed and pushed and tugged at each other, yelling in English or Arabic. No one made sense.

Hayne and I rushed into the melee — too close, I thought. I knew I was just about to see these young men kill the couple

or watch one of the Iraqis whip out a hand grenade, or draw us into a deadly ambush. It had all the makings of a trap — or a tragedy.

Capt. John Chau and Lt. Harry Thompson settled everybody down and sent the two Iraqis away with humanitarian rations, ending the crisis as quickly as it began.

We spent a sleepless night on that cold, muddy bank wondering if the couple behind us were grateful or if they would shoot us in the back.

For all the encounters that could have ended in tragedy, the ones that did were rare, and by the time we got to Baghdad, the Marines were no longer leaving so many bodies by the road.

ABOVE: First Lt. Harry Thompson, leader of Lima Company's fire support team, guides a mortar team into position to attack Iraqi snipers in a building in Qal'at Sukkar. (March 26)

FACING PAGE: Lt. Eli Vasquez scans the destruction on the road north of An Nasiriyah near Qal'at Sukkar. Vasquez, an artillery forward observer, was attached to Lima and rode in the commander's vehicle with the author and photographer. (March 26)

ABOVE: A wounded Iraqi soldier awaits medical attention from Navy corpsmen outside a bus where 18 Iraqi men and boys were killed by U.S. units the day before. It was not clear whether the unarmed Iraqi soldiers were deserting their units or heading south to reinforce other Iraqi Republican Guard units in the south. (March 27)

ABOVE: A dead Iraqi soldier is crammed against the dash of a bus that was shot by advancing Marine units north of Qal'at Sukkar. Eighteen Iraqis died in the bus. (March 27)

RIGHT: An Iraqi prisoner begs for his life after Marines find a sidearm in his bag during a patrol of a small village outside Al Hayy. When the man approached the patrol to surrender, he wore civilian clothes. Underneath the disguise, however, Marines found him dressed in a full Iraqi Republican Guard uniform. (March 29)

BELOW: Staff Sgt. Roy Whitener, 39, of Fresno, California, lights a cigarette for the prisoner and tries to reassure him that the Marine's won't execute him. (March 29)

ABOVE: An Iraqi man tells Marines that he is not the man pictured in military uniform in the photograph Marines found in his house while searching for weapons in Ash Shatra. (March 31)

LEFT: An Iraqi woman lay dead in the wake of a Marine surprise attack on Muwaffaqiyah. Marines said they mistook her for a sniper on the rooftop. Following the rules at the time, the Marines left her body where she fell. (April 2)

THIS PAGE: Marines check for survivors after a unit riddled a truck with bullets at a roadblock near Ash Shatra. An elderly Iraqi man was killed and a younger man, right, was seriously wounded when the two drove their car through a single coil of concertina wire the Marines had strung across the street. The Marines did not fire warning shots, and both men were unarmed. (April 1)

ABOVE: An Iraqi woman clutches her child as Marines search her house and surrounding buildings in a settlement outside Al Garaf. (March 25)

ABOVE: Navy Corpsman Richard Barnett of Camarillo, California, who aided an Iraqi soldier and is pictured here checking the wounded Iraqi girl's brother for injuries, said the situation was discouraging. "If there's anything good from this nonsense," he said, "I haven't seen it yet."

ABOVE: Navy corpsmen treat an Iraqi girl who was caught in the crossfire between Marines and Iraqi soldiers outside a village near Al Hayy. The girl was shot through the abdomen and wounded in the eye, her mother was killed, and her brother and father were wounded in the crossfire. (March 29)

BELOW: Marines lead her wounded father away from where his wife was killed.

FACING PAGE: First Sgt. Richard Grijava, of India Company 3/1, rushes the wounded girl to safety from the site of the tragedy.

ABOVE: Marines lead away an Iraqi prisoner near a village outside Al Hayy. Marines usually detained suspected soldiers or militia for hours and then sent them on their way with a humanitarian ration (yellow plastic bag). (March 29)

LEFT: Marines prepare to clear a rural settlement outside the town of Al Garaf during a sandstorm. (March 25)

ABOVE: Marines gather outside their vehicles minutes after crossing the Diyala River into Baghdad. An oil facility burns in the distance following several consecutive days of artillery bombardments and air strikes. (April 7)

FACING PAGE: Young Iraqi men walk south past a Marine convoy on the outskirts of Baghdad — a common sight as the Marines bore down on the capital. Marine officers said they believed that many of the men were soldiers deserting their units and fleeing the Marine advance. (April 6)

BAGHDAD: 48 HOURS

Use good judgement and act in the best interests of our Nation.
—Maj. Gen. James Mattis

WHAT THE MARINES CALL THE "PUCKER factor" is way up by the time we reach the outskirts of Baghdad on April 6.

Lumbering into a ghastly industrial district along the northeast edge of the city, we pass twisted wreckage of buses and enemy armor. Thousands of spent casings and bits of shrapnel litter the ground. Judging by a charred American tank, empty rocket tubes, and debris, the Iraqis had put up a hell of a fight.

We dig into a fallow wheatfield for the night. As I lay in my foxhole, the ground rumbles under the relentless bombardment from U.S. warplanes as they screech in and fire missiles and drop bombs. Iraqi and U.S. artillery batteries thump away in the distance, sending glowing rounds crossing over our heads. The reports are followed by series of distant explosions that rock and linger like rolling thunder.

At about 4 A.M. I see that Capt. Matt Reid is awake and pacing near the track, his radio handset pressed to his face as he talks in a hushed voice. He has a mission for Lima Company: In just a few hours, we will join the battle for Baghdad.

DAYBREAK, APRIL 7

In the darkness during a silent space in the barrage, I hear Arabic chants drifting from a distant mosque.

Our track commander gets up to take a leak.

If he's awake, I know it's time to get out of my sleeping bag and prepare to "stand to" — the ritual just before daybreak where we all stow our bedrolls and the track revs up as if we're about to go into battle.

Everyone's up now; our nerves are tweaked from all the explosions and gunfire nearby.

We don't talk about what's ahead, just mechanically prepare ourselves, each man lost in his own thoughts, listening to the chanting and waiting for more sounds of war.

8 A.M., APRIL 7

After meeting with Lt. Col. Lew Craparotta and the other company commanders, Capt. Reid gathers his four platoon leaders — young lieutenants in their late twenties.

They're going on what's called a leader's reconnaissance patrol along the Army Canal, which is all that separates us from Baghdad's eastern boroughs. On the patrol, Reid will show the officers where to position their platoons until the higher-ups determine if the bridges are too damaged for the convoy to cross the waterway. Hayne and I tag along.

We take off down a narrow trail with the officers. First Sgt. Timothy Ruff follows behind, watching over us. He always watches out for Hayne and me, but pretends like he's not doing it.

Tall grass rims the trail. Beyond it on both sides of the canal are muddy fields striped with deep furrows and surrounded by barbed wire and clusters of date palms. The sky is dark with low clouds and smoke. The air is still and steamy.

We move in formation, each man spaced about 20 feet apart and staggered on opposite sides of the trail. We expect contact.

It's beautiful, really, to watch soldiers on a tactical patrol. As the terrain opens up they instinctively spread out, and close in again when it narrows, always following the contours, always sticking close to something that shields them from full view. Hand signals freeze them in their tracks and, without discussion, they melt into the landscape like preying cats and wait silently for another signal before resuming the hunt.

The undulating course is a well-rehearsed dance that, if it becomes instinctive, saves lives in combat.

ZZzrrrrrrrrrrr — krunk! krunk! — Zzzzrrrrr — krunk! krunk! Artillery rounds screech in and slam into a building on the other side of the canal. Reid hits the dirt. We follow.

When you can hear the whine of incoming artillery rounds, you're too close. And when you can see them explode, then

you're way-too-goddamned-close. We were way-too-god-damned-close.

"Sounds like thunder," Cpl. Gunnar Schmitt says as we all crouch behind a berm facing the water.

The rounds slam into the buildings. Flames and black smoke gush from whatever was being hit. Machine-gun fire rattles from both sides of the canal.

"It's ours," Reid says. We trust him and keep moving.

1 P.M., APRIL 7

While the lieutenants position their men along the canal, we go back to the track and move out, stopping in the neighborhood where some of the fighting took place the night before. It's a ghost town, save for us and some of the battalion's officers, who are waiting for the battalion commander to finish his meeting with the commanding general.

Lt. Col. Lew Craparotta and Maj. Gen. James Mattis are inside the general's armored command track going over a plan to cross the Diyala River, a tributary of the Tigris River, which links with the canal just up the road.

We're told later that the bridges appear too badly damaged by U.S. artillery and airstrikes, so the battalion plans to secure some ground on our side, build a bridge, and then have Lima storm across to the other side.

Maj. Mike Lee, executive officer of the battalion, tells me the crossing makes us the most vulnerable so far. "It's one of the hardest operations for any military organization. It doesn't take much for the enemy to bottle you up when you cross. But we've got to do it, 'cause this is it. There's nothing left but Baghdad."

He stops, pausing for a minute while a volley of artillery rocks the neighborhood.

"Damn!" I say. "That's ours, right?"

"Yeah," Lee says. "They don't have anything left."

He continues looking into the distance, shaking his head slowly from side to side.

"C'mon guys," he pleads with the Iraqis he can't see, "just give up."

4 P.M., APRIL 7

Plans change and we all hustle back to the track.

We're going to swim across. Swim? In this thing?

It was risky. Although the tracks are designed to motor ashore from amphibious assault ships, it's never been tried after traveling as far overland as we have. I'm thinking about all the banging, rattling, and clanking that thing has done in the past couple of weeks. Can this track possibly be seaworthy?

Bolting across the neighborhood, we reach a steep embank-

ment where a long line of the regiment's tracks are splashing one by one into the foul-smelling water. They look like green crocodiles, just their tops visible above the water. They all seem to be making it to the other side. That's good.

The Marines in our track start pulling out cameras as we get to the water's edge.

The track gurgles and sputters, but we bobble along at a pretty good clip. Hayne, who was inside protecting his camera gear from water, jumps up top for a shot.

Marines cheer as we ford the river. A couple of enemy artillery rounds fly overhead but far from us.

The track climbs up the opposite bank, and water dribbles off our soaked packs like water off a wet dog.

"Freakin' Marines," blurts 1st Lt. Eli Vasquez. "We drive all this way and swim into Baghdad!"

Once across the river, we dig holes and spend the night in a field littered with burned-out trucks and unexploded rocket-propelled grenades. All night a drizzle falls. A nearby oil pump burns, its light pulsing off the smoke plume and the clouds overhead.

We wake up and immediately start patrolling the nearest neighborhood.

8 A.M., APRIL 8

After patrolling a nasty slum near the field where we slept last night, Lima Company moves on to clear a government-run power plant.

Several tracks line up side by side and crash through the 10-foot-high wall into the complex. Almost immediately shots are fired.

The rest of the company rushes in, Hayne and I with them.

After the Marines clear their way to the far end of the massive plant, Capt. Reid sets Lima up in the central courtyard at the entrance and orders the mortar men to start digging into a large grassy yard in front of a mural of Saddam Hussein.

Several tracks move to just inside the front wall of the yard and start firing .50-caliber machine guns at a few enemy soldiers firing back from some buildings about 900 meters across an open field. Capt. John Chau, the company executive officer, orders a sniper team to the roof of the main building to spot the enemy soldiers. Seeing some, Marines start firing almost immediately.

I follow some guys inside the building and snoop around.

It's a government plant, and this looks like the headquarters, with executive offices and portraits of Saddam Hussein and fat

Iraqi men in suits posing in front of portraits of the Iraqi leader. Inside, I run into a group of Marines walking out of a small room with their arms loaded with rolls of toilet paper and cans of Pepsi. Others follow with canned tuna, cheese spread, powdered milk, and other morale boosters.

I venture a little farther and find the ultimate morale booster.

First Sgt. Tim Ruff is in the plant director's office when I get there. His Kevlar helmet is off, and he's sitting in a big leather chair behind a huge hardwood desk trying to dial on the telephone.

I step beyond him, turn the corner, and let out a hoot, which he answers with a boyish laugh.

The plant director's personal shower is small and only trickles cold water, but after not showering in nearly a month it's a godsend. I run back to our track for my shaving kit and towel. I'm giddy.

Meanwhile, Marine snipers are on the roof firing a .50-caliber

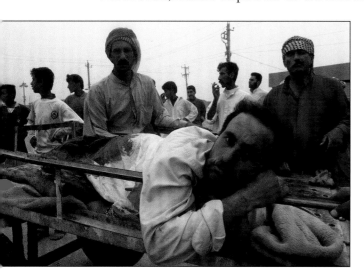

sniper rifle at a cluster of bunkers across the field. They set their looted Pepsi's aside and swallow the last of the cookies before taking aim and firing.

For about five glorious minutes, as Ruff stretches out on a leather sofa and snipers blast away on the roof, I scrub off three weeks of dirt. I laugh. I make silly noises. "Yooo hooo!" I re-soap and start all over again.

Soon Hayne is in on it, too, and while I dry off and put on fresh clothes, he showers and laughs and makes silly noises of his own.

It doesn't take long for the rumor of a shower to spread, and Marines soon line up to wash off their faces and hands before returning to the fight. More laughs. More silly noises.

The sink black and the floor slick, we leave like thieves.

"Rape, pillage, and plunder," Hayne mumbles, his mouth full of looted tuna and crackers.

3 P.M., APRIL 8

With a sledgehammer in his hands, Pfc. Anthony Roberts, 19, of Cincinnati, Ohio, climbs the steps to a 10-foot-tall color portrait of Saddam Hussein at the entrance to the power station. The first swing takes out the mouth and chin. Roberts hands the hammer to friend and cohort, Lance Cpl. Jeremy Steele.

Steele bashes the rest. They are following a 1st Marine Division directive to defile the image of Saddam.

"Relieving a little combat stress," Steele says, dropping the hammer and wiping the sweat from his forehead with a sleeve.

"We didn't get to shoot no rounds today," says Roberts, "but at least we got to beat on that."

I'm with the last group of Marines in the plant, and we load up and tear out of the power plant just as a mob of Iraqi looters crashes through the gates, arms waving and yelling like a pack of dogs. Within minutes, some of the buildings are in flames.

SUNSET, APRIL 8

We have to make it to Highway 5 by dark to link up with the other companies. Unlike the other methodical house to house searches, we briskly patrol through a mile of wretched slums intersected with streams of raw sewage and mounds of stinking rubbish. The object is to draw the enemy out.

One of the other platoons on our left flank takes sniper fire from an industrial complex a few blocks away near the highway.

As we rush toward the firefight, a group of men wheel a cart carrying a man badly wounded in the leg — apparently a bystander who was caught in the crossfire up the road. The Marines don't stop, drawing jeers and shaking fists from the men. The wounded man just glares as we walk away.

Ahead Marines are returning fire. They radio back to Reid that they've killed three shooters and taken two captive.

They bring the prisoners over to where we are, between a crowd of angry Iraqi men and a trash-filled field leading to the complex. Both men are wearing traditional robes — just like the growing crowd behind us.

Shots continue coming from the compound, so the Marines call in artillery and mortar fire. Several tracks line up in the field and blast the front wall of the compound with .50-caliber machine guns and 40mm grenades.

It's nearly dark, and explosions and flames light up the neighborhood when the Marines start hitting the several fuel tanks visible above the top of the wall. It isn't by accident; they are targeting the tanks.

We have no idea what kind of plant it is or what's inside the tanks. For all the noise about chemical and biological weapons being built at this site and that, it seems crazy to ignite these huge tanks with Marines and thousands of civilians all around — just to get a couple snipers.

It turns into an orgy of fire and howling as the Marines storm through a hole in the wall.

I look around me. I can't see Hayne. All I see are a couple hundred wild Marines rushing into the flames and a whole bunch of enraged Iraqis behind me.

I throw my hat in with the Marines and take off running toward the fire, where trucks were now exploding as the growing inferno touches off their gas tanks.

The air is thick with oily black smoke from whatever chemical is burning. About half of the 20 or so trucks are ablaze, and only a narrow gap stands between some of the flaming hulks and a brick wall. We sprint through just seconds before another truck explodes.

We don't find any snipers. More chemical tanks and trucks catch fire. Things explode in the distance behind us.

Thick black smoke chokes us as we reach the highway on the other side.

Hayne finally links up with us, climbing out of a track saying, "There you guys are."

All together again, we set in for the night.

A few of the guys venture into one of the houses nearest the track and find it vacant. Except for a few dog turds on the patio,

there were no booby traps in the house, and we deem it a safe place for the night.

We and the Marines are all exhausted and sleep on the roof of the house.

I lay awake, watching the clouds of smoke drift by, wondering what was achieved.

We wake before dawn to the chanted prayers from a neighborhood mosque, and no one speaks of yesterday.

ABOVE: Lima Company commander Capt. Matt Reid makes a radio check as artillery rounds strike nearby on the outskirts of Baghdad. (April 7)

FACING PAGE: A wounded Iraqi man and his friends plead with Lima Company Marines for help on a Baghdad street. Marines left the man and charged up the street to support another Lima Company platoon engaged in a firefight with snipers in a nearby industrial plant.

ABOVE: Lima Company commander Capt. Matt Reid, reclining with map, briefs leaders on a plan to build a bridge across the Diyala River to enter Baghdad. The Marines scrubbed the plan and within a few hours forded the river in their amphibious assault vehicles. (April 7)

ABOVE: Master Sgt. Keith La France guides assault vehicle drivers into position in a field littered with unexploded rocket-propelled grenades shortly after crossing the Diyala River. (April 7)

LEFT: After traveling nearly 1,000 miles over land, the Marines "float" across the Diyala River — a historic amphibious crossing. (April 7)

ABOVE: Marines cross a soccer field during a patrol of a neighborhood in eastern Baghdad. (April 8)

RIGHT: On the battalion's first full day in Baghdad, Cpl. Bryan Carter, left, and another Marine rush past an overturned Iraqi vehicle to help in a house-to-house search of a neighborhood. (April 8)

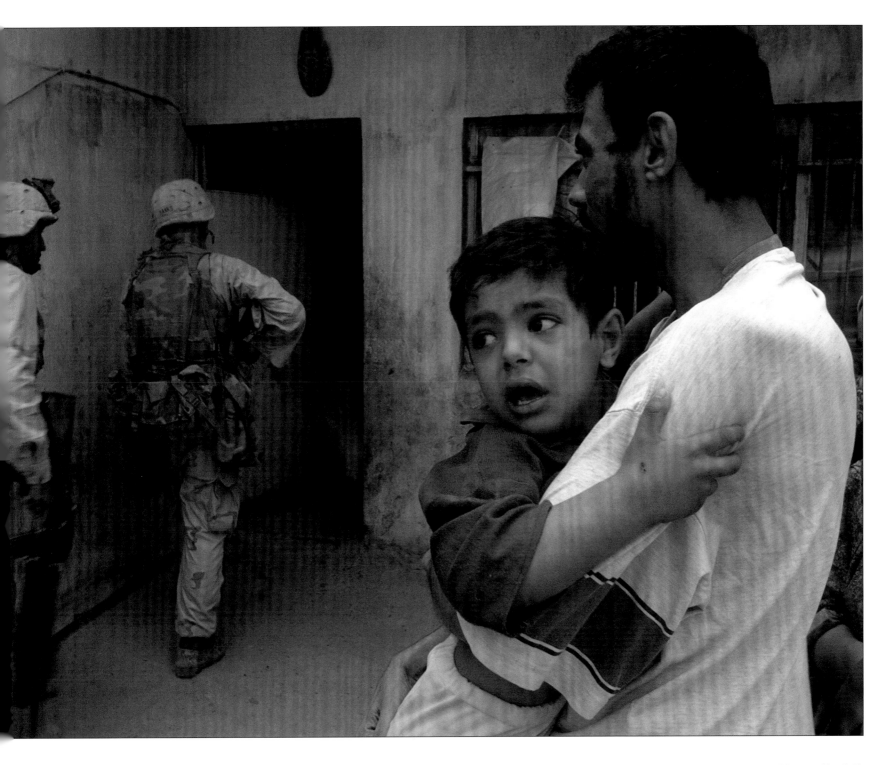

ABOVE: An Iraqi man holds his frightened son as Marines search his Baghdad home. (April 8)

ABOVE: Marines cover the main street through a Baghdad slum as other Marines search houses and vehicles for weapons. (April 8)

RIGHT: Cpl. Brian "Jeremy" Combs walks stone-faced past Iraqi women during a patrol of an eastern Baghdad ghetto. (April 8)

LEFT: Lance Cpl. Michael Redding attempts to urinate on a mural of Saddam Hussein at a power plant in Baghdad until his superiors call him off. (April 8)

ABOVE: An Iraqi man yells as he carries off a water fountain he looted from a Baghdad power plant. Looters tore into the plant as Marines pulled out and set the buildings ablaze. (April 8)

RIGHT: Iraqis loot appliances and fixtures from a government-run power plant that was temporarily occupied by the Marines. The looters took everything they could carry, and the Marines did nothing to stop them as long as they did not interfere with Marine operations. (April 8)

BELOW: In plain view of Marines, Iraqis haul off looted goods in eastern Baghdad. (April 8)

ABOVE: First Sgt. Timothy Ruff reclines on a leather couch in the director's office of a government-run power plant that the Marines temporarily occupied. (April 8)

RIGHT: Lima Company commander Capt. Matt Reid removes a portrait of Saddam Hussein from a wall in a conference room of a Baghdad power plant before briefing his men at the conference table. (April 8)

LEFT: An Iraqi prisoner who Marines said was an enemy sniper sings to calm himself as Marines rush past into a burning power plant. The Marines detonated several large fuel tanks in an attempt to kill other snipers thought to still be inside the plant. (April 8)

ABOVE: Lance Cpl. Joshua Zeller, 22, of Roll, Arizona, stands in front of an Iraqi crowd after patrolling through thousands of cheering residents of Saddam City for more than three hours. The crowds were so thick and uncontrollable that the Marines had to flee the neighborhood. (April 10)

FACING PAGE: An Iraqi man gives a thumbs up and sells a Marine a soda outside Nu'maniyah. Up to this point in the war, this was the friendliest and closest Iraqis and Marines had come without incident and it signaled the beginning of the unexpected welcome by Iraqis in the streets of nearby Baghdad. Marines heard erroneous radio reports that day indicating that Saddam Hussein was held under house arrest by a mutinous Republican Guard unit. And although a serious tank battle had been fought just up the road in Aziziyah earlier that day, many Marines said they believed the war was nearly over. Note: The contrail above them is from a B-52 bomber turning around outside Baghdad without dropping its bombs. (April 4)

Unexpected Welcome

While we will move swiftly and aggressively against those who resist, we will treat all others with decency, demonstrating chivalry and soldierly compassion for people who have endured a lifetime under Saddam's oppression.
—Maj. Gen. James Mattis

THE LAST THING I EXPECTED TO SEE IN Baghdad were happy children bearing flowers.

Rubble and lots of dead Iraqis were about all I could imagine.

But on April 9, when we arrived in Baghdad's biggest neighborhood — the massive slum of Saddam City, home to half of Baghdad's 6 million residents — we rode in on a wave of celebration and goodwill.

The Marines could hardly hold them back: Iraqi men and boys swarmed around the tracks as Marines struggled to erect roadblocks and barriers to keep them out.

"We didn't expect them to love us so much," said Cpl. Joshua Stallbauh, 25, of Pasco, Washington. "But I guess I can see why if we are giving them something they've wanted for years."

Men chanted "Good Bush! Good Bush," and the kids chirped, "Mista! Mista!" over and over.

Men and boys offered us cigarettes, and neighbors invited troops in for tea. One man offered me

whiskey, and Cpl. Armando Davila won the attention of a teenage girl, who flirted with him through a doorway until her father chased her inside.

Their cars stacked with stolen wares, looters drove by the obstacles, honking and waving as if to say "thank you."

The residents of the city were celebrating their liberation from Saddam Hussein. Their lives had changed forever.

From Lima's patch of grass at the edge of a sandy field near the central soccer stadium, Hayne and I gathered with a few Marines around our crank-up shortwave radio to listen to BBC reports of similar celebrations throughout the city.

Commentators said U.S. forces had pulled down a statue of Saddam Hussein in Fardus Square in front of several dozen Iraqis and dozens more journalists who were staying in the nearby Palestine Hotel.

More chaos followed.

Iraqis poured from homes to greet the Marines on our first foot patrol on April 10.

First a trickle, then a flood of Iraqis engulfed the tracks and the Marines as we pushed down the streets. The locals chanted, skipped and clapped, and followed us tirelessly for hours, handing Marines bouquets and wreaths and asking our names. The kids cheered when we'd respond, then they'd run ahead to meet us again and ask the same question.

Hayne and I got separated in the rush of people. I climbed a pole to try to spot him, but I couldn't see him and could barely make out individual Marines in the flow. It looked like the tracks were floating down the street on a river of colorful, dancing Iraqi people.

When too many people got too close to the Marines, we retreated to the tracks and headed back to our camp, where I eventually found Hayne. Exhausted and bewildered by the warm welcome, the Marines contemplated a much different mission than the combat role they had trained for.

ABOVE: Sgt. Daniel Coleman, from Seattle, Washington, gets a surprise kiss from an elated resident of Aziziyah. Residents chanted "Good Bush!" and "Long life (sic) Bush!" as the Marines patrolled the streets. (April 5)

ABOVE: Iraqis wave and cheer Marines as they drive around Saddam City celebrating the fall of Saddam Hussein. (April 9)

LEFT: An Iraqi man helps a Marine drag a sandbag from an Iraqi bunker into a Saddam City street to build a roadblock to keep other Iraqis away from the Marines' vehicles. (April 9)

ABOVE: Pfc. Anthony Roberts, 19, from Cincinnati, Ohio, holds back a crowd in Saddam City. (April 10)

RIGHT: Pfc. Jason Scanlon, 21, of Port Charlotte, Florida, is hugged by Iraqis in Saddam City. (April 10)

ABOVE: An Iraqi girl hands Lance Cpl. Lloyd Williams of Georgetown, South Carolina, a rose at a barricade in Saddam City on April 9. Military leaders soon forbade Marines from such exchanges after Army soldiers and Marines were killed and wounded by suicide bombers in similar crowds. (April 9)

RIGHT: Marines often disobeyed the order and decorated their uniforms and vehicles with flowers and wreaths given them by Iraqi children. (April 9)

ABOVE: A crowd swarms around Marines standing outside an amphibious assault vehicle in Saddam City. Marines were vulnerable to attack in crowds and soon had to restrain the Iraqis and gain some distance. (April 10)

RIGHT: Pfc. Dusty Snowden, a combat engineer, shoos away an aggressive crowd in Saddam City. Although they said they were happy about the huge welcome, many Marines soon tired of the crowds and forced them back, sometimes swinging their rifle butts and yelling at them to make the point. (April 10)

LEFT: Cpl. Ryan Brown of Visalia, California, is swarmed by Iraqi children during a patrol of the Al Quds neighborhood in Baghdad on his 23rd birthday. "I wish I was home partying for my birthday," he said. "But I guess being here helping these people isn't that bad." (April 20)

RIGHT: Iraqis fill the streets to greet Marines in Saddam City. The uncontrollable crowds frustrated the Marines, who often became separated in the mass of people. (April 10)

BELOW: Exhausted and overwhelmed, Marines escape the aggressive Iraqi crowds in their amphibious assault vehicle and head back to a protected camp near the central soccer stadium in Saddam City. (April 10)

ABOVE: Lima Company executive officer Capt. John Chau scares away an Iraqi looter from a Baghdad power plant that the Marines temporarily occupied. The Marines had no orders at the time to stop looters, but some Marines, including Chau, said it was un-American to allow looting and did their best to stop it. (April 8)

"THIS IS NOT MARINE BUSINESS"

Chemical attack, treachery, and the use of the innocent as human shields can be expected, as can other unethical tactics. Take it all in stride.
—Maj. Gen. James Mattis

WE QUICKLY DISCOVERED THAT BAGHDAD HAD A DARK SIDE: the night.

As dusk carpeted Iraq's capital city, the Marines abandoned their patrols, pulling out of the neighborhoods to the relative safety of our camps.

They left the streets to gangs, looters, and resistance fighters.

And gunfire. Unremitting gunfire.

"I don't like it. It isn't home," Lance Cpl. Darrin Duhon, 19, of Abbieville, Louisiana, told me after a particularly nerve-rattling night. "People all the time shootin' from every side. Last night we had rounds comin' over our heads while we were sleeping. All you hear is choong, choong, choong. It's freaky."

Night made it clear that U.S. forces had not subdued the city.

At first, military officials said the gunfire was celebratory. The reality was that other forces were at work in the city, ones that the Marines had not counted on and did not yet understand. But they were reluctant to become the new sheriff in town.

During the day the Marines patrolled neighborhoods where residents begged them to do something about the violence at night.

"This is not Marine business," Capt. Matt Reid told a group of Iraqis pleading for the Marines to stay during the night. He threw his arms up. Frustrated, he wanted to help, but orders were orders.

Privately, some officers said the nocturnal gunmen were probably the same ones killing and wounding Marines at roadblocks and in ambushes around the city.

One local man called them "the ones with beards."

"In the night, we are exposed to the fires of the men who work for Saddam Hussein. We put impediments in the road, but we need more," he said, explaining that "foreigners" were driving trucks through his neighborhood firing weapons as soon as the Marines left and held the residents hostage until they returned.

When local Shiite Muslim clerics said they had the guns and the men to do what the Marines seemed unwilling to do, the Marines handed over Saddam City.

More accustomed to taking ground than giving it up, the Marines reluctantly pulled back. And from their new camp at the edge of Saddam City, all the Marines could do was listen to the gunfire and wonder.

RIGHT: Iraqis cart away office furniture looted from a government building in Baghdad as Marines approach from behind. The Marines drove past the looters and continued their mission hunting down Iraqi fighters. (April 8)

ABOVE: An Iraqi man pleads with Marines to stop the Iraqi-on-Iraqi violence in his neighborhood of Saddam City. Code-named "Chicago," an agent of the U.S.-trained Free Iraqi Forces, left, translates the man's concerns to Capt. Matt Reid. "Chicago," a 43-year-old former Iraqi Army officer, later slipped away from the Marines and was sought by military officials in Baghdad. (April 11)

RIGHT: An Iraqi woman watches and weeps as Marines pass her Baghdad home. She told the Marines that they should leave Iraq. (April 11)

ABOVE: An angry Iraqi doctor leads Marines on a patrol of his hospital in Saddam City. The doctors asked the Marines to leave and said they were outraged when the Marines refused. The doctor, who spoke English, called the intrusion "abuse." (April 10)

ABOVE: Marines stand by and watch as Iraqi looters clear out an office building in Baghdad. The Marines had no plan for the frenzy of looting in the wake of the invasion, and it was weeks before they were ordered to stop it. (April 8)

RIGHT: Cpl. Bryan Carter confronts an Iraqi medic trying to cross Marine lines to treat Iraqi civilians who were injured when a weapons cache exploded. While Baghdad's poor cheered the Marines, professionals and English-speaking, middle-class residents often cursed them for not providing basic services and security after the invasion. (April 14)

ABOVE: An Iraqi woman peers out of her black cloak at Marines after alerting them of a huge arms cache in her neighborhood. Squatters were using unexploded artillery and tank main gun rounds as building materials and furniture. (April 18)

ABOVE: Iraqis burn tires and trash at night to light the streets as they try to protect themselves and their possessions from looters and armed gangs fighting for power in Saddam City. While they eventually set up night ambushes, the Marines generally did not patrol the city at night. (April 19)

RIGHT: An elderly woman leads Marines to her Baghdad neighborhood where Iraqi soldiers had stockpiled artillery rounds. (April 20)

ABOVE: An Iraqi Muslim leader pleads with Capt. Matt Reid to protect his neighborhood from looters and militia who shot at residents and homes at night after the Marines left Saddam City for their camp. "This is not Marine business," Reid told the man. (April 9)

ABOVE: A Marine radioman patrols a street in Saddam City. (April 11)

FACING PAGE: Marines find cover during a raid on one of Saddam Hussein's bunkers, already gutted by fire. (April 14)

Walking Baghdad

Keep faith in your comrades on your left and on your right. Fight with a happy heart and a strong spirit.
—Maj. Gen. James Mattis

AS THE TRACK GROWLED TO A STOP, A YOUNG Marine banged an ammunition magazine against his helmet to set the bullets forward.

Sweat rolled down the sides of his dirty, stubbled face, making little muddy tracks along his jawbone where his chin strap soaked it up. He didn't look at what he was doing — he just stared down at his boots.

He slammed the magazine into the receiver of his M-16 and smacked it again for good measure. He yanked back the charging handle, let it go, and chambered a round with a loud clack.

A series of clicks and clacks filled the belly of the track as the other Marines followed suit.

No one said a word or looked at each other except for Sgt. James Regan, 27, of San Antonio, who sang a country-western song in a Texas drawl through a wad of Copenhagen and then cracked wise about Iraqis.

"Mista! Mista!" he said, mocking the refrain the Iraqi children pestered the Marines with on every patrol. The kids were already right outside.

Light and dust flooded the chamber as the ramp yawned open.

Pointing their weapons out into the busy Baghdad street, the Marines charged out left and right into oncoming traffic, some aiming their weapons at stunned drivers, others scanning rooftops and windows, storefronts and doorways, their rifles held chest high.

It was another day, another patrol down another Baghdad street.

For two weeks, Lima and the Marines from the battalion's other companies walked Baghdad's northeastern suburbs, every day making mad dashes in the tracks to different parts of town for surprise foot patrols through the neighborhoods.

Mounting up in the looted industrial yard the Marines turned into a defensive base, they rolled out the gates onto a main street in a cloud of dust and headed for who-knew-where. Hayne and I usually tagged along.

The Marines called them "saturation patrols" — a show of force to reassure the "good" Iraqis and flush out or scare away the "bad guys."

The Marines were always followed by chattering Iraqi children bearing flowers and cigarettes and eager to strike up conversation, but the charm of being "liberated" was wearing off on many residents, and Iraqis started to demand that order and basic services be restored.

The patrols bore mixed results.

While the patrols provided a good way to meet the residents, the Marines rarely found any "bad guys," and they had neither the know-how to restore services nor the manpower to provide general security. The Marines also had neither the time nor the means to safely transport and dispose of the dozens of huge arms caches abandoned in civilian neighborhoods and schools by the Iraqi forces.

Walking around for hours through the streets and revisiting the arms stockpiles, the Marines were roaming targets for terrorists and punching bags for Iraqis who wanted their lives back.

"Tell Mr. Bush that what we need is water. What we need is bread. We need lights!" said one elderly man as he walked past a patrol, swinging a plastic bag of flat bread, yelling at a group of Marines.

Others were more pointed in their criticisms of the American invasion.

"You weren't invited here," said a man who was a science professor at the University of Baghdad until U.S. bombers blew up his labs and classrooms. His comments emboldened a small crowd gathered in front of a hospital, where Iraqis were asking the Marines for protection. They closed in and nodded at everything he said.

"They make a great plan for war. But why did they not think of what will happen after Saddam Hussein? After the American army destroyed our country, our system?

"You make a good plan for war. You make a good plan for the oil fields, and American embassy and British embassy — but nothing for the people of Iraq," he said. "Us, you leave to thieves. I tell you, you are the thieves."

ABOVE: A Marine inspects piles of assault rifles, rocket-propelled grenades, and ammunition collected by Lima Company during patrols in Baghdad. The Marines confiscated small arms and weapons that could easily be used against them but left the stockpiles of bombs and munitions for the Iraqis to deal with. (April 13)

RIGHT: Marines burst into a gutted Iraqi military bunker during a raid and are surprised to find the complex empty. (April 14)

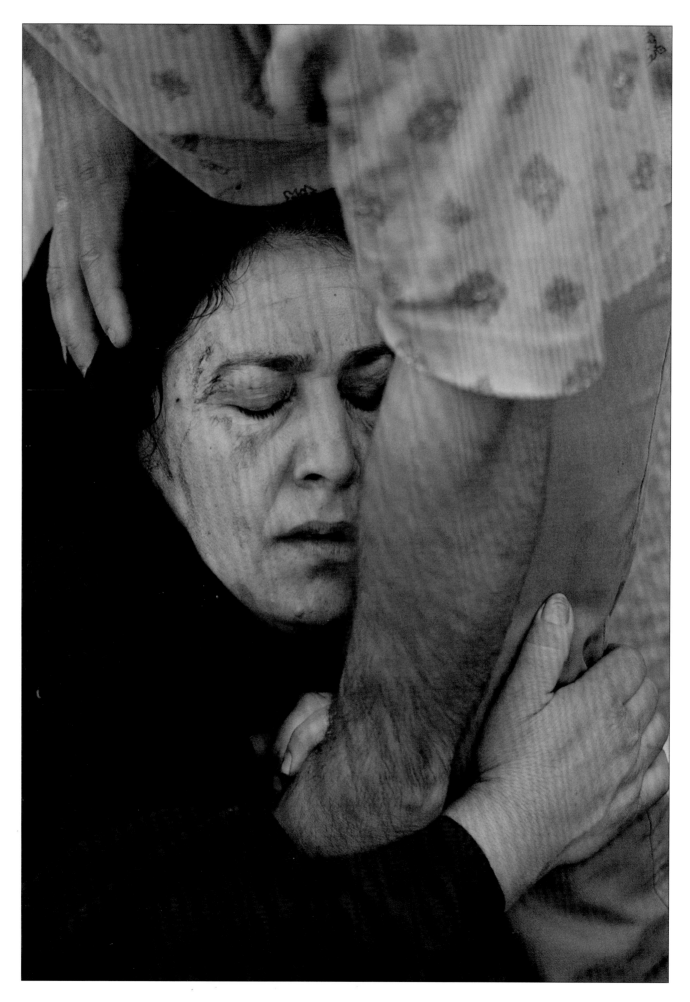

TOP: Marines rush in to investigate and help the wounded when a huge stock-pile of Iraqi munitions stored in some newly built homes explodes in a nearby neighborhood. According to some residents, children who were playing with the ammunition were killed when it exploded. (April 14)

ABOVE: Marines look up to see the plume seconds after the weapons cache explodes.

LEFT: Neighbors help an Iraqi man who was wounded with shrapnel after a secondary or "cook-off" blast. The Marines left the wounded Iraqis, and continued patrolling other neighborhoods.

FACING PAGE: A neighbor comforts a woman who was wounded in the blast.

ABOVE: Marines remove a cache of small arms from a Baghdad school and detain a man who was armed with an AK-47. (April 14)

RIGHT: Waiting for a Catholic Mass to begin on Palm Sunday, a Marine holds his head in his hands after a long patrol. Head in hands was a common pose for the weary Marines during their final days in Baghdad. (April 13)

ABOVE: Iraqi girls watch as Marines rummage through their family's Baghdad home looking for weapons and military uniforms. (April 10)

ABOVE: Exhausted after five weeks of war and a long march out of Baghdad, Reserve Master Sgt. Keith La France, 53, takes a minute to rest along the road between Al Hillah and Diwaniyah. The assault vehicle he commanded — the one that transported Lima Company's commander, forward observers, and the author and photographer through Iraq — finally broke down near here after traveling more than 1,000 miles from Kuwait through southern Iraq. (April 22)

FACING PAGE: Mail finally reaches the Marines at their camp in an industrial yard in Baghdad, and they take time out to see what they are missing back home. (April 16)

Ordinary Men

Demonstrate to the world that there is "no better friend, nor worse enemy" than a U.S. Marine.
—Maj. Gen. James Mattis

WHEN LIMA COMPANY FINALLY MADE IT HOME to Camp Pendleton from Iraq at about 3 A.M. on May 23, 2003, Hayne and I were there to greet them.

It was an assignment — we had to write a story and shoot pictures — but we were also there as friends.

We'd returned home a month earlier, leaving Lima on April 26 on a Marine helicopter back to Kuwait, and from there, back to San Diego on a commercial flight a few days later.

The Marines had sat for most of the month, trying to keep their sanity in 120-degree heat in a former Iraqi military base in Diwaniya, about 80 miles south of Baghdad.

Arriving home, they all looked skinny and sunburned. They had

lost some of the hard warrior armor and grit that I remembered, and they now looked like very tired, very ordinary men. They melted into the arms of loved ones.

After all the hugs and kisses, tears and cheers of the emotional homecoming, some of the Marines gathered in one of the offices in the barracks. They invited Hayne and me in for the beer we'd all promised each other in Iraq if we made it back alive.

Gunnery Sgt. Wayne Hertz, one of the guys we were closest with over there, was going to make the toast. Hertz had returned a week earlier than the rest of the guys in Lima to prepare the barracks for the single Marines. He'd already bought a

new truck and gotten reacquainted with his wife and two kids. And he didn't have that shell-shocked look that hung on everyone else like a death in the family.

"Well, here's to America! Here's to the flag!" Hertz said, raising a can of Coors Light.

"Hear, hear!"

I said it, but I was a bit bewildered.

The entire time we were in Iraq, through all the fear and fighting, hard work and horseplay, I had never heard anyone wax patriotic.

From Camp Inchon in Kuwait, over the berm at the border, through southern Iraq and into Baghdad, they spoke not a word about flag or country.

They talked about simple stuff. It was all about brothers and friends. All about families and loved ones at home. All about Lima and 3/1.

But I understood Hertz.

He had had a week home to try to make sense of it all, to put it all together in categories and stories that explained, ordered and justified the experience.

Just as I was, he was editing.

Details that didn't fit, things that offended or troubled or didn't make sense, were pushed back and the story was cleaned up, made straight, packaged for retelling.

And after telling it a few times — because everyone wants to know "what was it like?" — it's tidy, with a beginning and an end, a few central themes and the best stories up front. It all makes sense. It has meaning.

In place of pure memory, what you're left with is the echo of how you told it the last time, bounced off the walls of what you've learned since. Behind the walls lay memory.

Going back to my notes about the war, I came across a story that seemed like just an odd detail at the time, but now sums up the experience.

On a house-to-house search for weapons in Muwaffaqiya, the Marines kicked open a door to a vacated home, finding the usual bed mats on the floor, wads of Iraqi currency, a couple of AK-47s, and portraits of Shia martyrs and Saddam Hussein.

Returning to the yard, they found a door to a small shed or closet and forced it open. They were outraged at what they found.

"C'mere, you guys, you gotta see this," a Marine called out. We soon followed more Marines into the yard.

Inside the cell sat a strangely beautiful Iraqi woman chained by the neck to a concrete wall.

None of us knew who she was, who chained her there, or why. We couldn't really tell if she was a woman or a girl.

She didn't react. She didn't resist. She sat there silently rocking back and forth on a pile of wool blankets, looking frightened and very far away.

The Marines did what they thought was the obvious and right thing: They cut her chains.

Gunnery Sgt. Jerry Yates, a gruff, stubby track leader, grabbed a pair of bolt cutters the Marines had been using to force their way into homes.

Yates was a real piece of work: always in need of a shave and always wearing his helmet cocked to the side and the chin strap undone. He was straight out of a Bill Mauldin cartoon or a Norman Rockwell painting — and you could easily see him in black and white telling a handsome Robert Mitchum: "Aye Aye, sir, consider it done!"

Full of American idealism and armed with a sharp pair of bolt cutters, Yates and the others did what any U.S. Marine would do — they freed her from her chains.

But then, without knowing what would come next — how she'd fend for herself, if her oppressor would return, or what fate awaited her — they nodded and patted each other on the backs for a good deed done and moved on. Hayne and I documented it, and we did the same, leaving the woman in the yard, alone.

When the Marines pulled out of Baghdad three weeks later and camped in a field outside of Al Hillah, near the ruins of ancient Babylon, the battalion's mission was done. And with that, Hayne and I ended our assignment as embedded reporters.

For a day and a night as we all said our goodbyes, exchanged addresses and took our final group shot, a constant stream of U.S. Army vehicles drove past us on the highway — heading north toward Baghdad.

The constant rattling and groaning of thousands of tanks and howitzers and troop transports heading north into Iraq nagged at us from the background, somewhat spoiling the satisfaction of being done with the war.

Like a chore left undone, or an untidy fib, the clatter of an army heading north robbed the victory; it stole the ribbon we all wanted to tie up the war with.

We still don't know what became of the Iraqi woman without her chains.

ABOVE: Cpl. Gunnar Schmitt naps with his new friend "Willie," a puppy that Lima Company's Marines adopted at an industrial yard where they spent their last nine days in Baghdad. (April 16)

ABOVE: Navy chaplain Lt. Wayne Haddad blesses some of Lima Company's officers during a Catholic Mass celebrated in an abandoned Baghdad warehouse on Palm Sunday. From front to back: Company commander Capt. Matt Reid; 1st platoon leader, 1st Lt. Greg Jones; 3rd platoon leader, 1st Lt. Donald Toscano. (April 13)

RIGHT: Gaunt and tired, 1st Lt. Harry Thompson hangs his head during a rest in Baghdad. (April 15)

ABOVE: Lance Cpl. Dawud Sabata, 20, from the Bronx, New York, rests and smokes, passing time as the battalion's mission dries up after two weeks in Baghdad. The Marines made a home in the rubble of a looted and abandoned industrial yard for nine days before they finally pulled out of Baghdad on Easter Sunday. (April 20)

RIGHT: In a quiet, solitary moment when Lima Company's Marines get letters from home for the first time. Pictured are Gunnery Sgt. Wayne Hertz, center; Capt. Andrew Clevenger, left; 1st Lt. Eli Vasquez, right. (April 11)

FACING PAGE: Coming home. After waiting with families for hours, Marianne Poole kisses her husband, 1st Lt. Kevin Poole, when Lima Company arrives back at Camp Pendleton before dawn. (May 23)

RIGHT: Marines from Lima Company call home after returning to Camp Pendleton. The Marines from the 3/1 were the first "grunts" — or Marine infantrymen — to return to the base from the war. (May 23)

ABOVE: Group shot. The author, photographer, and some of the company they kept. This photo was taken in Al Hillah, about 60 miles south of Baghdad. (April 22)

RIGHT: Happy to finally get home together, jubilant Marines pile on top of one another after being dismissed for a four-day leave after arriving home to Camp Pendleton from Iraq. (May 23)